LEWIS & CLARK

THE CORPS OF DISCOVERY

JOHN HAMILTON

VISIT US AT
WWW.ABDOPUB.COM

Published by ABDO & Daughters, an imprint of ABDO Publishing Company, 4940 Viking Drive, Suite 622, Edina, Minnesota 55435.

Printed in the United States.

Edited by Paul Joseph
Graphic Design: John Hamilton
Cover Design: Mighty Media
Photos and illustrations:
    John Hamilton, p. 1, 5, 6, 8, 11, 12, 15, 16, 20, 22, 24, 26, 27, 28
    American Philosophical Society, p. 25
    Beinecke Museum, p. 17
    Buffalo Bill Historical Society, p. 21
    Independence National Historical Park, p. 9
    Library of Congress, p. 5, 18, 19, 30-31
    Missouri Bankers Association, L. Edward Fisher, p. 4
    National Archives, p. 20
    New York Historical Society, p. 14
    Charles Willson Peale, p. 13, 23
    Olaf Seltzer, p. 7

Library of Congress Cataloging-in-Publication Data

Hamilton, John, 1959-
    The Corps of Discovery / John Hamilton
    p. cm.—(Lewis & Clark)
    Includes bibliographical references and index.
    Summary: Joins the Lewis and Clark Expedition in the spring of 1804 as they set out to explore the Louisiana Purchase. Includes highlights and directions to historical points of interest.
    ISBN 1-57765-761-6
    1. Lewis and Clark Expedition (1804-1806)—Juvenile literature. 2. West (U.S.)—Discovery and exploration—Juvenile literature. 3. West (U.S.)—Description and travel—Juvenile literature. 4. Lewis, Meriwether, 1774-1809—Juvenile literature. 5. Clark, William, 1770-1838—Juvenile literature. [1. Lewis and Clark Expedition (1804-1806) 2. West (U.S.)—Discovery and exploration. 3. Lewis, Meriwether, 1774-1809 4. Clark, William, 1770-1838.] I. Title.

F592.7.H257 2002
917.804'.2—dc21

2001053395

TABLE OF CONTENTS

"Honored Parence,

"I am now on an expidition to the westward, with Capt. Lewis and Capt. Clark… through the interior parts of North America. We are to ascend the Missouri River with a boat as far as it is navigable and then go by land, to the western ocean, if nothing prevents…

"We expect to be gone 18 months or two years. We are to receive a great reward for this expidition, when we return.

"I… will write next winter if I have a chance."

SERGEANT JOHN ORDWAY

THE CORPS OF DISCOVERY

*I*n the spring of 1804, a keelboat and two oversized canoes loaded with 47 men and supplies crossed the Mississippi and entered the mouth of the Missouri River, straining against the swift and muddy current. The explorers called themselves the Corps of Discovery. They were young men entering uncharted lands. At the request of President Thomas Jefferson, they were beginning the most important expedition in the history of the United States. Led by two remarkable commanders, they would travel thousands of miles through plains filled with vast herds of wild animals, across rugged mountains, and down rivers teeming with fish.

Prairie grass on the Great Plains, North Dakota

Bison grazing on the Great Plains of North Dakota

They would meet dozens of Indian tribes, many of whom had never before seen white men. The expedition was armed with the most advanced weapons of the time. But though expedition members would tell the Native Americans their land was no longer their own, expedition members would be met more often by kindness than hostility, generosity more than mistrust. Several times, when the expedition was on the verge of destruction, these soldier-explorers would be saved by the compassion of others.

They would be the first American citizens to gaze upon the vastness of the Great Plains; first to cross the Continental Divide; first to struggle over snow-capped peaks until they reached rivers that ran westward. Following these, they would be the first American citizens to reach the Pacific Ocean overland from the east.

Two U.S. Army officers, very different from each other, led the Corps of Discovery. Captain Meriwether Lewis was the commander, the planner, the scientist. Captain William Clark was the steady one, the mapmaker, the leader of men. They were both superb woodsmen. They were great friends, and their skills complemented each other perfectly. Within a few months they molded their men into an efficient unit that followed orders and carried out tasks with precision. The men of the Corps worked as a team, and they would follow Lewis and Clark anywhere.

After more than 8,000 miles (12,875 km) and nearly two and a half years of exploration, the Corps of Discovery would fail in its mission to find the fabled Northwest Passage, the easy, long-sought trade route to the Pacific Ocean. But Lewis and Clark succeeded in bringing back a wealth of discoveries—122 new kinds of animals, 178 new plants. They made contact with dozens of native tribes. They strengthened the United States's claim on the North American continent. And just as importantly, the Corps of Discovery fired the imagination of a nation. They blazed the trail that would soon be followed by legions of trappers, traders, and settlers.

The Lewis and Clark expedition is a story of dedication and courage, friendship and teamwork. It's the story of America.

Artist Olaf Seltzer painted this scene of Meriwether Lewis climbing a ridge on May 26, 1805. "From this point," Lewis wrote, "I beheld the Rocky Mountains for the first time."

"*However our present interests may restrain us within our own limits, it is impossible not to look forward to distant times, when our rapid multiplication will expand itself beyond those limits and cover the whole... continent, with a people speaking the same language, governed in similar forms and by similar laws.*"

THOMAS JEFFERSON
FIRST INAUGURAL ADDRESS

Look Forward To Distant Times

On March 4, 1801, Thomas Jefferson took office as the third president of the United States. The young country contained just over five million people—20 percent of those were African-American slaves. Two-thirds of American citizens lived within 50 miles (80 km) of the Atlantic Ocean. Settlers were pushing westward beyond the Appalachian Mountains, but there were only a handful of roads reaching into the new territories. There were no telephones or telegraphs. Letters and packages traveled at the speed of a horse, sometimes taking weeks to reach far-off destinations. United States territory ended at the eastern banks of the Mississippi River.

Beyond the Mississippi, reaching all the way to the Rocky Mountains, lay a vast and largely unknown area called Louisiana. First

claimed by Spain, then given to the French, Louisiana represented Napoléon Bonaparte's great hope of a worldwide empire reaching into the Americas. But nobody really knew what was in Louisiana. Scattered Indian tribes lived there; only a few fur trappers had ever ventured into its outer edges.

Thomas Jefferson knew that his young country's destiny depended on exploring the unknown lands west of the Mississippi River.

To the south and west, New Spain stretched from Florida to Texas, all the way to the California coast. England controlled territory to the north, in Canada. English traders and trappers were already starting outposts, pushing into Minnesota and the Dakotas. English ships cruised up and down the coastlines of the Pacific Northwest, and Russians were building forts in Alaska. All of these countries wanted to control the western reaches of the North American continent. Whoever won the race would lay claim to all the riches and vast opportunity of that unknown land.

After the American Revolution, there were at least four attempts to find the headwaters of the Missouri River. Once found, the explorers would seek a short portage over low mountains until reaching the Columbia River, which flows west to the Pacific Ocean. (Most people assumed the hike would be like crossing the Appalacian Mountains. Actually, the Rocky Mountains are much more rugged. Some western peaks soar twice as high as Virginia's Blue Ridge Mountains, which were thought at the time to be the highest on the continent.)

Thomas Jefferson, one of America's Founding Fathers, organized three of these expeditions to explore the continent's interior. None of them succeeded. A young Virginian by the name of Meriwether Lewis once volunteered, but he was turned down because he was only 18 years old.

President Thomas Jefferson was a brilliant politician. He was also a scientist with a great thirst for knowledge. At his Virginia home, Monticello, he collected a vast library. He was especially interested in natural history, delighting in the discovery of new plants and animals.

In Jefferson's library were many books on the unexplored regions of North America. He owned more books on the subject than any library in the world. The books told of woolly mammoths, erupting volcanoes, and hills of pure salt. The books also spoke of the fabled Northwest Passage, a mostly water route that cut through the continent, making it easy to send trade goods from coast to coast.

Jefferson had a grand dream that the United States would someday occupy the entire continent. He wanted to create a single nation, governed by democracy, which stretched from coast to coast. Jefferson knew that commerce and trade would be the driving force to achieve his dream.

Like many people at the time, Jefferson believed the Northwest Passage existed. It would open up the country to fur traders and others who were eager to make money in the rich markets of the Orient. Without an easy overland route, eastern traders had to send ships on a long and dangerous journey, either around southern Africa or the tip of South America.

Jefferson knew that whichever country occupied the unexplored lands west of the Mississippi had a better chance of laying claim to them. This is why there was such a great push to explore, to get fur trapping established, and to make trading alliances with Native American tribes.

In 1793, Scotsman Alexander Mackenzie explored the southern reaches of Canada. He managed to cross the Continental Divide and make it to the Pacific. Mackenzie's explorations gave the British a toehold on the western regions, but his route wasn't very useful for trade because of the rugged mountain areas that had to be crossed.

Alarmed that the British had a head start exploring the inner continent, Jefferson proposed yet another expedition. It would be headed by his personal secretary, Meriwether Lewis, the young man who years earlier had volunteered for one of Jefferson's other ill-fated expeditions. This time, Lewis was old enough to go. He would blaze a trail through the heart of a continent.

"Capt. Lewis is brave, prudent, habituated to the woods, & familiar with Indian manners & character. He is not regularly educated, but he possesses a great mass of accurate observation on all the subjects of nature which present themselves..."

THOMAS JEFFERSON
LETTER TO DR. BENJAMIN RUSH, FEBRUARY 28, 1803

MERIWETHER LEWIS

*I*n early 1801, the presidential election was so close that Congress had to decide who won. Just before inauguration day, a divided Congress chose Thomas Jefferson over his bitter rival Aaron Burr. Once in office, Jefferson, a Republican, found himself surrounded by his political enemies, the Federalists. He needed someone he could trust as his personal secretary.

Meriwether Lewis was a young man in his late 20s. He grew up in Albemarle County in Virginia, not far from Jefferson's home, Monticello. Like Jefferson, Lewis was the son of a plantation owner. As with most Virginia plantations at the time, the main crop was tobacco, and the fields were worked by slaves.

When Lewis was a young boy of five, his father died serving in the Colonial Army during the American Revolution. His mother soon remarried and moved the family to her new husband's estate in Georgia.

Lewis loved the outdoors. He learned to fish and hunt by the time he was eight. He was moody and serious, self-reliant and sturdy. Although he was a fearless horse rider, he also loved to "ramble," walking endlessly through the woods. His mother taught him about wild plants that could be used as medicine. Through her, Lewis gained a love of learning.

Meriwether Lewis, in a painting by Charles Willson Peale. Lewis's outdoor skills and sharp powers of observation convinced Thomas Jefferson that the young Virginian was the right man to lead the Corps of Discovery.

Lewis knew that he needed an education, that someday he would be responsible for the family's plantation. However, there weren't many schools back then. Many children of rich plantation owners went to live with teachers for a time. So, when he turned 13, Lewis moved back to Virginia and lived with a tutor. He loved to read. He studied botany, history, math, and geography. Although he still loved to roam alone in the woods, he worked hard at his studies.

After five years of schooling, Lewis was forced to stop his education. His mother's husband had died, and she needed assistance moving herself and Lewis's siblings back to the family plantation in Virginia. After helping her move, Lewis found himself in charge of the estate.

Taking care of a 2,000-acre (809-ha) plantation was a huge responsibility, and Lewis threw himself into it. He worked hard to make sure land was cleared, crops were planted and harvested, and all the day-to-day routines were taken care of.

Meriwether Lewis poses for artist Charles de Saint-Mémin after returning from the wilderness in 1806. The fur cape that he wore, which Lewis called *"the most eligant peice of Indian dress I ever saw,"* was a gift from Shoshone chief Cameahwait. The cape was made of otter skin trimmed with white weasel fur. The Corps visited the Shoshone tribe while camped near the Continental Divide in what is today southwestern Montana.

Though he worked hard, the life of a Virginia plantation owner didn't suit Lewis very well. He wanted to roam in the woods again, to get out where he could spread his wings and explore. When he was 20, he joined the military. Lewis served as a United States Army officer on the wild frontiers of Pennsylvania and Ohio, honing his skill as a sharpshooter while traveling up and down the Ohio River.

In 1801, Thomas Jefferson called Lewis to Washington, D.C. The president hired the 28-year-old Virginian to be his personal secretary. Jefferson chose Lewis because he was a friend, a neighbor, and a good Republican, a rarity in the army. Jefferson wanted to get rid of Federalist officers that former President John Adams appointed before leaving office. Jefferson had no army experience himself. Lewis, on the other hand, knew which officers would be loyal to the president.

As the president's sole aid, Lewis met some of the most powerful and influential people in the country. He also learned much of Jefferson's interest in the West, and the potential held in that immense, unexplored territory.

Thomas Jefferson's home, Monticello, in Albemarle County, Virginia. Meriwether Lewis grew up near Monticello. He also spent time there while serving as the president's aide, planning the Corps of Discovery.

"*To Captain Meriwether Lewis.*

"*The object of your mission is to explore the Missouri river, &
such principal stream of it, as, by it's course and communication
with the waters of the Pacific ocean... may offer the most direct &
practicable water communication across this continent for the
purposes of commerce.*"

THOMAS JEFFERSON

THE OBJECT OF YOUR MISSION

As Thomas Jefferson's personal secretary, Meriwether Lewis lived in the newly constructed White House for two years. During this time, the building was called the President's House. Later, the British burned the residence during the War of 1812. The residence was repainted a bright white, which is why it is known today as the White House.

Jefferson was recently widowed, and his two daughters were grown and married. Lewis stayed in the East Room of the mansion. He ran errands for the president, copied official papers, and made lists of army officers he expected to remain loyal to Jefferson. Aside from the servants, Lewis and Jefferson were the only people to occupy the President's House. Lewis dined with the president nearly every night. Jefferson once wrote, "Capt. Lewis and myself are like two mice in a church."

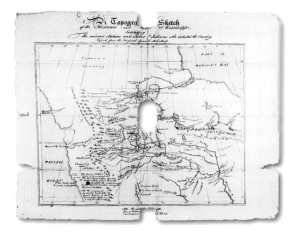

A Topographic Sketch of the Missouri and Upper Mississippi, by Antoine Soulard, in 1802, correctly showed the Missouri River heading toward the Rocky Mountains. Soulard was wrong, however, in representing the mountains as a single line of small bumps on the map. Thinking the Rockies to be a minor obstacle, Thomas Jefferson was determined to send the Corps of Discovery farther west than any expedition had ever before ventured, into the blank western areas of the map, the great unknown.

One hundred years after the Lewis and Clark expedition, photographer Edward S. Curtis made it his life's work to roam the West, documenting Native American culture. He took this image of Ogalala Sioux chief Red Hawk in the South Dakota Badlands in 1905.

Lewis learned the thorny details of diplomacy and politics during his stay with Jefferson. He rubbed elbows with Washington's elite, from powerful congressmen to foreign diplomats. As they grew closer, Jefferson became a father figure to Lewis. The president noted that Lewis was prone to bouts of depression which Jefferson called "depressions of the mind." But his confidence in the young Virginian never wavered.

On January 18, 1803, Jefferson sent a confidential letter to Congress. "The river Missouri," he wrote, "and the Indians inhabiting it, are not as well known as is rendered desirable... An intelligent officer with ten or twelve chosen men... might explore the whole line, even to the Western Ocean."

Jefferson made the expedition more attractive to his Federalist rivals by emphasizing commercial gain. He also kept the cost low, only $2,500 to fund the entire expedition, although the cost would eventually climb to $38,722. On February 28, 1803, Congress approved the president's proposal. Jefferson was delighted. He chose his young aide, Meriwether Lewis, to lead the expedition. Lewis eagerly accepted.

Some people thought it was odd that Jefferson picked someone like Lewis to lead so important an expedition, but the president was confident in his choice. Jefferson wrote that Lewis was "brave, prudent, habituated to the woods, & familiar with Indian manners & character."

Over the next several months, Jefferson and Lewis made plans. Lewis would take several dozen men on a military mission Jefferson called the *Corps of Discovery*. Besides searching for the Northwest Passage, the expedition had several other goals. Expedition members would collect and describe plants and animals they discovered. They would map rivers and mountains, along with precise latitude and longtitude measurements. They were to note the land's economic potential—how well it could be farmed, and if it contained precious minerals, such as gold or silver. They were also to contact Indian nations, record their cultures and customs, and bring them into a trade partnership with the United States.

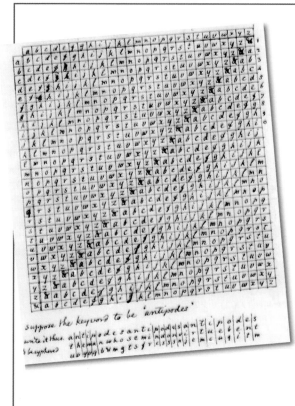

Thomas Jefferson worried that messages sent back from the Corps might be intercepted, especially by the English or Spanish, so he created this code matrix for Lewis to use. To decode a message, the sender and receiver decided in advance on a secret keyword, in this example, "antipodes." By knowing the keyword, the receiver could then look up the corresponding letters on the grid and unscramble the message.

To test the code matrix with Lewis, an optimistic Jefferson wrote, *"I am at the head of the Missouri, all well, and the Indians so far friendly."* Despite taking this precaution, no records have been found of Lewis sending a coded message back to Thomas Jefferson.

Lewis made many lists of supplies the expedition would need to complete its journey. This list details the guns, ammunition, and some of the clothing Lewis bought for the men of the Corps.

Jefferson sent Lewis to Philadelphia, Pennsylvania, to train with some of the country's best scientists. Lewis learned how to preserve plant specimens, how to measure latitude and longitude, and how to identify fossils. He also learned medicine from one of the most famous doctors of the time, Dr. Benjamin Rush, who taught Lewis the importance of "bloodletting." By opening a sick person's vein and releasing blood, it was thought that toxins would be flushed away. Of course, today we know that this only makes matters worse, but at the time everyone believed that bloodletting helped most illnesses.

While in Philadelphia, Lewis kept busy collecting supplies for the expedition. The men would be completely out of touch with civilization for at least two years. Lewis purchased some preserved soup, but the men would have to hunt for most of their food. Lewis bought the most modern rifles available at the time, the Model 1803, the army's first standard issue rifle. Lewis also bought an air rifle with his own money. The weapon was much like today's BB gun, but more powerful. He would amaze the Indian tribes with its power and accuracy.

Lewis bought compasses, a telescope, and a chronometer, used to make accurate readings of the expedition's

A reproduction of the compass used by William Clark to collect daily readings of distance and direction. He used these readings to draw a map of the West for President Jefferson. Today, the original compass is in the Smithsonian Institute in Washington, D.C.

Lewis & Clark

longitude. He also purchased other supplies, such as tent cloth, pliers, saws, hatchets, medical supplies, fishing hooks, 12 pounds (5 kg) of soap, 45 flannel shirts, shoes, woolen pants, blankets, knives, 500 rifle flints, and lead to make bullets.

Lewis also bought presents to give to the Native Americans they expected to meet. The gifts included mirrors, sewing needles, brightly-colored cloth, colored beads, tobacco, and bright red vermilion, which was prized for making face paint.

Lewis also purchased 600 "Rush's Thunderbolts," powerful laxative cure-alls. Dr. Rush was convinced that by inducing severe diarrhea, a patient could expel toxins that caused illness. Like bloodletting, it was exactly the wrong treatment to give a sick person. But, as historian Stephen Ambrose noted, it sure kept the men's insides cleaned out.

By the time he was finished, Lewis had bought over 3,500 pounds (1,588 kg) of supplies. But he knew he needed something else: a co-commander to help lead the expedition. He also knew just the man for the job.

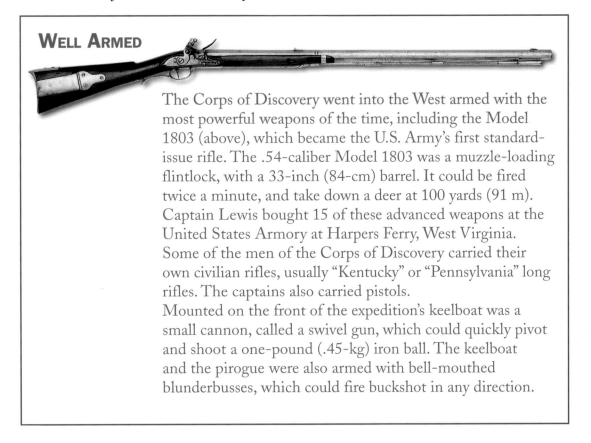

WELL ARMED

The Corps of Discovery went into the West armed with the most powerful weapons of the time, including the Model 1803 (above), which became the U.S. Army's first standard-issue rifle. The .54-caliber Model 1803 was a muzzle-loading flintlock, with a 33-inch (84-cm) barrel. It could be fired twice a minute, and take down a deer at 100 yards (91 m). Captain Lewis bought 15 of these advanced weapons at the United States Armory at Harpers Ferry, West Virginia. Some of the men of the Corps of Discovery carried their own civilian rifles, usually "Kentucky" or "Pennsylvania" long rifles. The captains also carried pistols.

Mounted on the front of the expedition's keelboat was a small cannon, called a swivel gun, which could quickly pivot and shoot a one-pound (.45-kg) iron ball. The keelboat and the pirogue were also armed with bell-mouthed blunderbusses, which could fire buckshot in any direction.

June 19th, 1803
Dear Clark,
My friend... If there is anything in this enterprise, which would induce you to participate with me in it's fatiegues, it's dangers and it's honors, believe me there is no man on earth with whom I should feel equal pleasure in sharing them as with yourself.

MERIWETHER LEWIS

Dear Lewis,
This is an undertaking fraited with many dificulties, but My friend I do assure you that no man lives whith whome I would perfur to undertake Such a Trip.

WILLIAM CLARK

WILLIAM CLARK

fter buying supplies, Lewis prepared to return to Washington, D.C. By this time, he had decided he needed a co-commander: his old army buddy William Clark. Maybe Lewis felt overwhelmed at the task he was taking on. Perhaps Lewis needed help directing the men of the Corps, given his bouts of depression. Or maybe Lewis simply needed a friend for the long trip to come. Whatever the reason, Lewis wrote to Clark, inviting him to join the Corps of Discovery.

William Clark, although born in Virginia, had spent most of his life on the wild frontiers of Kentucky and Ohio, learning to fight and negotiate with Native Americans. Clark had once been Lewis's army commander. They had worked together for only six months, but in that time had grown to be great friends.

Clark, a sturdy, red-headed man, was four years older than Lewis. He wasn't as educated, but had more practical experience in the military. He had a steady and calm personality. He was outgoing and confident, an inspired leader of men. Where Lewis might get upset about a situation, Clark would remain calm and think his way out of the problem. Their skills complemented each other, and they trusted one another completely.

In a letter to Clark, Lewis broke with tradition and asked his friend to be co-commander of the expedition. Clark quickly accepted Lewis's offer.

In the military, it's very unusual to split command. The army refused to go along with their plan. When Clark's commission finally arrived, it was as a second lieutenant, not captain. Lewis was embarrassed. He insisted that he and Clark keep the matter a secret, and always referred to Clark as captain. They would be equals throughout the expedition.

William Clark, painted by Charles Willson Peale

"*The sale assures forever the power of the United States, and I have given England a rival who, sooner or later, will humble her pride.*"

NAPOLÉON BONAPARTE, 1803
COMMENTING ON THE LOUISIANA PURCHASE

INTO THE UNKNOWN

*I*n late summer 1803, Lewis had a 55-foot (17-m) keelboat made near Pittsburgh, Pennsylvania, on the Ohio River. From there he would float the expedition's supplies down the Ohio, picking up Clark along the way. They were heading to St. Louis, where the Corps would spend the winter of 1803-04. On the way, Lewis and Clark would handpick the best men available to join the Corps of Discovery. The men would come from all walks of life. Most had military experience, but many were civilians, including hunters, and French trappers to row the pair of big canoes, or pirogues, that would follow alongside the keelboat.

Just before Lewis left Washington to head west, something unexpected happened. It would have a huge impact on the Corps of Discovery's mission.

William Clark's map of the Great Falls of the Columbia River

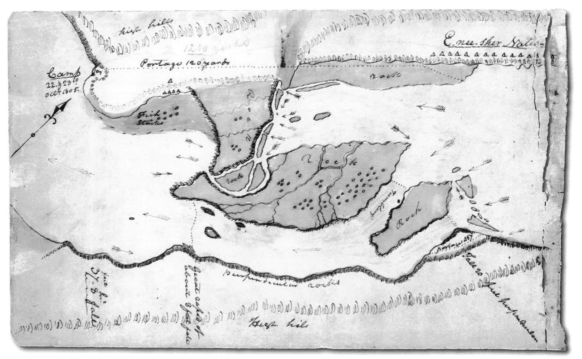

Artist Bob Scriver sculpted this statue of Meriwether Lewis, William Clark, and Sacagawea. The young Indian woman joined the expedition during their winter stay at the Mandan villages in present-day North Dakota.

In 1802, President Jefferson had sent diplomats to France. He wanted to buy New Orleans, which was an important French-controlled port at the mouth of the Mississippi River. Whoever controlled New Orleans controlled river traffic on the Mississippi. If the United States wanted to expand westward and set up trade, it needed free access to the Mississippi. There were only a few roads back then; rivers were the superhighways of the time.

Instead of selling New Orleans, Napoléon Bonaparte made a counteroffer: he would sell the entire French-controlled Louisiana Territory, all 820,000 square miles (2,123,798 sq. km). France was at war with England, and badly needed money. The $15 million Napoléon wanted would help the war effort. He also knew that he could never put enough soldiers in Louisiana to stop the westward migration of American settlers. He would lose the territory anyway. He reasoned that by selling the entire territory, he could pick up some badly needed cash, plus it would help make the United States a great power that would rival England.

Napoléon declared that by selling the entire Louisiana Territory, he had "strengthened forever" the United States. "I have given England," he said, "a rival who, sooner or later, will humble her pride."

Jefferson jumped at the chance to buy Louisiana, paying a mere three cents per acre for the land. With one deal he had nearly doubled the size of the United States.

Not everybody liked the purchase, however. Jefferson's political enemies thought it was a horrible waste of money ($15 million was nearly twice the federal budget at the time). The Boston *Columbian Centinel* wrote, "A great waste, a wilderness unpeopled with any beings except wolves and wandering Indians. We are to give money of which we have too little, for land of which we already have too much."

But Jefferson was sure the Louisiana Purchase would greatly strengthen the young nation. He was one step closer to realizing his dream of spreading democracy from coast to coast. The Corps of Discovery would now be exploring American territory.

On July 4, 1803, the news of the purchase was announced. The trouble was, most of the map of Louisiana Territory was a big blank. What was out there? Were there really woolly mammoths, erupting volcanoes, and mountains of pure salt, as Jefferson's books foretold? Louisiana Territory was a huge unknown, a true mystery.

The next day Meriwether Lewis left Washington, D.C., for St. Louis. The Corps of Discovery was on its way. Lewis and Clark would soon see for themselves what lay in that vast, unexplored land.

A thunderstorm produces a rainbow on the plains of Montana near the Rocky Mountains.

IF YOU GO TODAY

A flower garden on the west side of Monticello

MONTICELLO

Thomas Jefferson's domed house, Monticello, is one of the most distinctive buildings in America. Jefferson was an amateur architect who planned and supervised every detail in the construction of his mountaintop home.

Situated in Albemarle County, near Charlottesville, Virginia, Monticello is part of a 5,000-acre (2,023-ha) plantation that Jefferson inherited when he was 14 years old. The grounds surrounding his home were devoted to Jefferson's personal garden, a living laboratory where he studied plants from around the world. Today, the vegetable garden shares space with flower gardens, a fruit garden, orchards, vineyards, and a multitude of trees, Jefferson's favorite garden plants.

Jefferson was constantly upgrading and remodeling Monticello. He began construction in 1768. He completely remodeled it starting in 1796, and finished by the time he retired from public life in 1809. Today, Monticello is recognized as an international treasure, the only house in America on the United Nations' World Heritage List of sites to be protected at all costs.

Guided tours inside Monticello are entertaining and revealing. The entrance hall contains many American Indian artifacts and natural history specimens, including several from the Lewis & Clark expedition.

Monticello is open every day of the year, including Sundays, except Christmas. It is located two miles (3.2 km) southeast of Charlottesville, approximately 125 miles (201 km) from Washington, D.C., and 110 miles (177 km) from Williamsburg, Virginia. Tickets entitle visitors to a 30-minute guided tour of the home, access to the Museum Shop, and self-directed tours of the grounds. Guided tours of the gardens and grounds are also available. For more information, contact the Thomas Jefferson Memorial Foundation at (804) 984-9822, or write to: Monticello, Department of Public Affairs, P.O. Box 217, Charlottesville, VA, 22902.

American Philosophical Society

The American Philosophical Society is the nation's oldest scholarly society, founded in Philadelphia, Pennsylvania, by Benjamin Franklin in 1743. Thomas Jefferson sent Meriwether Lewis here to learn from the nation's top scientists before embarking on the Corps of Discovery. Most of the Lewis and Clark journals, along with other artifacts from the expedition, are housed at the Society's headquarters building, located in Independence National Historical Park, around the corner from Independence Hall and the Liberty Bell.

Exhibitions in Philosophical Hall and Library Hall are open to the public. For more information, write to: American Philosophical Society, Library Hall, 105 South Fifth Street, Philadelphia, PA 19106-3386, or call (215) 440-3409.

GLOSSARY

CHRONOMETER

A scientific instrument used to measure time precisely. By knowing the exact time and measuring the position of the sun, Lewis and Clark were able to make accurate readings of the expedition's longitude, the distance east or west on the earth's surface.

CONTINENTAL DIVIDE

A ridge of the Rocky Mountains in North America. Water flowing east of the divide eventually finds its way to the Atlantic Ocean. Water flowing west goes to the Pacific Ocean.

CORPS

A branch of the military that has a specialized function.

DEPRESSION

An emotional condition, often caused by a chemical imbalance in the brain, that causes feelings of hopelessness and sadness. Meriwether Lewis likely suffered from bouts of depression.

FEDERALIST PARTY

A political party in the U.S., from 1789 to 1816, that favored a strong, centralized government. Alexander Hamilton and President John Adams were prominent Federalists.

FLINTLOCK

An old-fashioned rifle or pistol in which a flint in the hammer strikes a piece of metal, which produces a spark that ignites the gunpowder.

GREAT PLAINS

A huge, sloping region of valleys and plains in west-central North America. The Great Plains extend from Texas to southern Canada, and from the Rocky Mountains nearly 400 miles (644 km) to the east.

HEADWATERS

The beginning of a large stream or river.

Lewis & Clark

KEELBOAT

A large, shallow-hulled freight boat used extensively in the 18th and 19th centuries on the Mississippi and Missouri Rivers.

NORTHWEST PASSAGE

The fabled easy water route across North America from the Atlantic to the Pacific Ocean.

PIROGUE

A large, canoe-shaped boat used to carry cargo, that is powered by oars, or sometimes a sail. The Corps of Discovery used two pirogues to supplement the larger keelboat on the journey up the Missouri River in 1804. In 1805, the pirogues continued upriver as far as Great Falls, Montana.

PORTAGE

To carry a boat and supplies overland from one lake or river to another. It can be a difficult and grueling process, depending on the terrain.

REPUBLICAN PARTY

A former U.S. political party formed by Thomas Jefferson. (Today's Republican Party was formed in 1854 to oppose the extension of slavery.)

VERMILION

A bright red powder, made of mercuric sulfide, that is used as a pigment. Native Americans used it to make face paint, trading with white settlers for the prized powder. Native Americans had their own methods of making red pigment, but vermilion powder was easiest to obtain and use.

WEB SITES

Would you like to learn more about Lewis & Clark? Please visit **www.abdopub.com** to find up-to-date Web site links about Lewis & Clark and the Corps of Discovery. These links are routinely monitored and updated to provide the most current information available.

INDEX